ENERGY FOR THE FUTURE AND GLOBAL WARMING

# GEOTHERMAL ENERGY

## By Nigel Saunders

Consultant: Suzy Gazlay, M.A.,
science curriculum resource teacher

**Gareth Stevens**
Publishing

Please visit our web site at: www.garethstevens.com
For a free color catalog describing Gareth Stevens Publishing's
list of high-quality books, call 1-800-542-2595 (USA) or
1-800-387-3178 (Canada).

Library of Congress Cataloging-in-Publication Data available upon
request from publisher.

ISBN 978-0-8368-8400-5 (lib. bdg.)
ISBN 978-0-8368-8409-8 (softcover)

This edition first published in 2008 by
**Gareth Stevens Publishing**
A Weekly Reader® Company
1 Reader's Digest Road
Pleasantville, NY  10570-7000  USA

This edition copyright © 2008 by Gareth Stevens, Inc.

Produced by Discovery Books
Editors: Geoff Barker and Sabrina Crewe
Designer: Keith Williams
Photo researcher: Rachel Tisdale
Illustrations: Stefan Chabluk and Keith Williams

Gareth Stevens editor: Carol Ryback
Gareth Stevens art direction and design: Tammy West
Gareth Stevens production: Jessica Yanke

Photo credits: Photodisc: / cover, title page, 7, 14. National Park Service: 9.
DOE / NREL: / Warren Gretz 17; / David Parsons 23. istockphoto.com:
/ Mark Owens 18; / Lukas Hejtman 21.

Printed in the United States of America

1 2 3 4 5 6 7 8 9 11 10 09 08 07

# CONTENTS

**Cover photo:** Old Faithful geyser in Yellowstone National Park, Wyoming, erupts regularly — about every ninety minutes.

Words in **boldface** appear in the glossary or in the "Key Words" boxes within the chapters.

# CHAPTER ONE

# ENERGY AND GLOBAL WARMING

Energy fills the universe. It is everywhere, even inside you. Electricity is one kind of energy, but there are many other kinds. Some are easy to see. We can see light energy, hear sound energy, and feel heat energy. Anything that moves has kinetic energy.

The Sun bathes our planet with huge amounts of energy that keeps us warm. It also gives plants the light they need to make their own food. We are not so aware of other types of energy. These are stored in a number of different forms. Food and fuels store chemical energy. When you squash a ball or stretch a rubber band, it stores **elastic energy**. As we will see, a lot of energy is also stored as heat in the ground beneath our feet.

Energy can be changed from one form to another. We can make electricity using sunlight, wind, or the power of water. Very little electricity is made in these different ways, however. Most of the electricity we use is made from **fossil fuels**.

## Fossil fuels

Oil, natural gas, and coal are fossil fuels. They took millions of years to form from the buried remains of dead plants and animals. Fossil fuels store chemical energy. When they burn, fossil fuels release their energy as heat.

## ENERGY USE IN THE UNITED STATES IN 2005

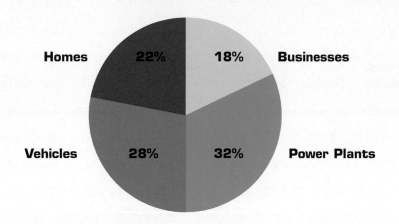

| | |
|---|---|
| **Homes** 22% | 18% **Businesses** |
| **Vehicles** 28% | 32% **Power Plants** |

This chart shows energy use in the United States. It shows how much was used by homes, businesses, **power plants**, and vehicles.

Gasoline and diesel are fuels made from oil. They power our cars and trucks. Natural gas provides heat for cooking and heating. Coal generates half the electricity needed in the United States. About two-thirds of all the world's electricity is made using coal and the other fossil fuels. The United States has one-fourth of the world's coal reserves (fuel still in the ground). Coal supplies may last more than two centuries.

Fossil fuels will not last forever. They will get used up. They are not **renewable** energy resources. It would take millions of years for new fossil fuels to form. People need to find other sources of energy.

> "The reason geothermal is a good alternative energy is that it's a good twenty-four-hour cycle. The Sun goes down at nighttime, the wind doesn't blow all the time, but the steam comes from the Earth all the time."
>
> U.S. Senator Harry Reid, Democrat; Nevada (2006)

## Pollution

There are other reasons to avoid using fossil fuels. They give off smoke and harmful gases as they burn. These **emissions** cause pollution. Emissions are harmful substances given off that pollute land, air, or water.

Chemicals from fossil fuels get into rain, sleet, and snow. When it rains or snows, the chemicals in the moisture can harm plants. When people talk about acid rain, they mean any precipitation that contains acidic chemicals from fossil fuel emissions. The chemicals can kill entire forests.

Pollution from cars and factories also hangs in the air over some large cities. The emissions form smog, a thick, dirty chemical fog that causes illnesses.

## Global warming

Fossil fuel burning also gives off **greenhouse gases**, such as carbon dioxide and water vapor. Greenhouse gases trap heat in the atmosphere. They keep Earth warm enough for living things to exist. When too much heat is trapped, Earth gets warmer than usual.

## EFFECTS OF GLOBAL WARMING

The amounts of greenhouse gases in the air have increased in the last one hundred years. Scientists believe this increase is causing Earth to get warmer. This changes the worldwide weather patterns, or climate. The climate change is called **global warming**.

Even small rises in temperature cause big weather changes. Some places get too much rain. Others get too little. Large sheets of ice melt into water and cause ocean levels to rise. Governments around the world are taking the advice of scientists on how to reduce or even stop global warming.

Icebergs form when large chunks of a glacier or an ice shelf break away into the ocean. This iceberg is in Paradise Bay, Antarctica.

## GEOTHERMAL ENERGY

| GOOD THINGS | PROBLEMS |
|---|---|
| Provides energy day and night, all year long | Most places do not have access to geothermal water |
| Geothermal power plants take up only a small amount of land | Release of steam from geothermal power plants can be noisy |
| Renewable but heat can be removed faster than it takes to quickly reheat | Rocks become cold if too much heat is removed too quickly and take a long time to reheat |
| Clean | Power plants give off low levels of carbon dioxide (16 percent of that produced by natural gas) |

Scientists believe we can help slow global warming by reducing our use of fossil fuels. We must produce lower amounts of greenhouse gases.

### Geothermal energy— clean and renewable

To reduce our use of fossil fuels, we must look for other, cleaner sources of energy. **Geothermal energy** is a clean source of energy. The word geothermal comes from two Greek words. "Geo" means "earth" or "ground." "Therme" means "heat." So, "geothermal" means "heat from the ground."

The rocks inside Earth store a lot of heat energy because of natural processes deep underground. These processes are always going on. The heat energy stored inside Earth is renewable energy. It will not run out, no matter how much we use it.

In some places, geothermal energy stored in the ground comes to the surface. People and animals have always used this released energy for warmth. These bison (buffalo) gather at a hot spring in Yellowstone National Park, Wyoming. The water that bubbles up at this place is naturally heated by the hot rocks below.

For thousands of years, people have used geothermal energy. Today, scientists are exploring new ways to use this energy from the ground.

## KEY WORDS

**fossil fuels:** fuels formed in the ground over millions of years, including coal, oil, and natural gas

**global warming:** the gradual warming of Earth's climate

**greenhouse gases:** gases in the atmosphere that trap heat energy

**renewable:** having a new or reusable supply of material constantly available

# CHAPTER TWO

# HOT ROCKS

Our planet, Earth, is a rocky planet. It is not just solid rock, however. Earth has three main layers. The outer layer is a thin, solid **crust**. Underneath the crust is a layer called the **mantle**. The very center of Earth is called the **core**.

You would have to dig down almost 4,000 miles (6,400 kilometers) to get to Earth's center. Earth's core is made from a mixture of iron

## EARTH'S LAYERS

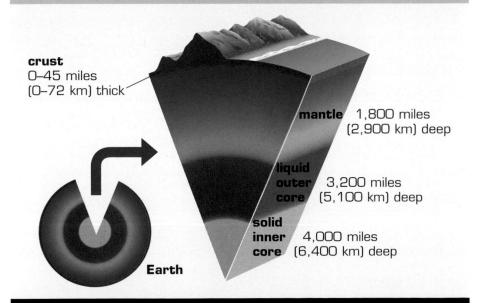

**crust**
0–45 miles
(0–72 km) thick

**mantle** 1,800 miles
(2,900 km) deep

**liquid outer core** 3,200 miles
(5,100 km) deep

**solid inner core** 4,000 miles
(6,400 km) deep

**Earth**

Earth has a layered structure. The layer we live on, the crust, is the thinnest layer. Earth gets hotter the deeper you go.

## EARTH'S CORE

The deeper you go underground, the hotter it gets. This is not because of fires deep inside Earth. Instead, much of the heat energy comes from **nuclear reactions**. A nuclear reaction is a change that takes place in the center of an atom (one of the tiny particles that makes up all things). Earth's core contains substances that produce nuclear reactions. Huge amounts of heat energy are released when those nuclear reactions happen. That heat rises up through the mantle and crust. It warms Earth from the inside out.

and nickel. It has two layers. The inner core is under so much pressure that it is solid. It is also very hot. The inner core is believed to be about 7,000 degrees Fahrenheit (3,900 degrees Celsius). The outer core is under less pressure. It is liquid and a little cooler.

The mantle is made of rock layers. Heat from the core melts the lower part of the mantle. The lower mantle layer is so hot it stays melted, or molten. Like any liquid, this molten rock can flow. But the mantle is so thick and flows so slowly that you would never notice the movement.

Earth's crust is made of rock, too. This rock is solid, and it is the layer we live on. The crust is as thin as 3 miles (5 km) under the oceans and up to about 45 miles (72 km) thick elsewhere. People have never drilled all the way through Earth's crust.

## Earth's plates

Earth's crust and the top, solid layer of the mantle are broken into huge slabs of rock called **tectonic plates**. The North American plate is the world's fourth-largest plate. It is so big that Canada, Greenland, and Iceland — and nearly all of the United States and Mexico — are on it.

Even though these plates are huge, they move all the time. Plates drift gradually, like pieces of ice floating on a slow-moving river. The plates move only a few inches (centimeters) per year. They travel at about the same speed that your fingernails grow! Over millions of years,

this movement adds up. Continents that were once joined together have moved thousands of miles apart.

The movement of plates is not always smooth, even when plates just slide past each other. Sudden movement of plates causes earthquakes. Breaks in the crust — called faults — form where plates meet. They can shift or slide.

## Hot spots

Underground temperatures are higher along the lines where tectonic plates meet. High underground temperatures can also be found in regions where Earth's crust is thin. In these parts of the world, magma (hot, molten rock) rising through the crust causes **hot spots**. Alaska, California, Oregon, and Nevada all have hot spots.

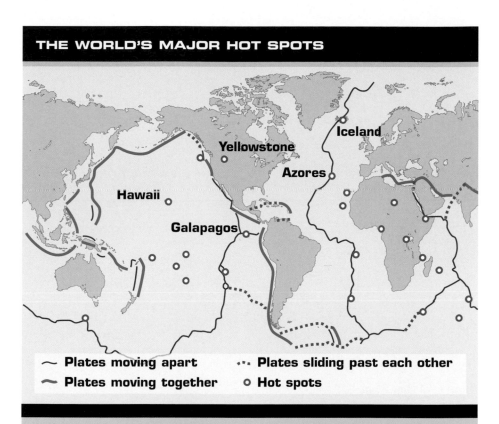

## THE WORLD'S MAJOR HOT SPOTS

Iceland
Yellowstone
Azores
Hawaii
Galapagos

~ **Plates moving apart**       ... **Plates sliding past each other**
~ **Plates moving together**     o **Hot spots**

This map shows some of the world's major hot spots. Notice that many of them occur at the edges of tectonic plates. Some of them — like the Hawaiian Islands hot spot — are located in the middle of a tectonic plate.

The Hawaiian Islands formed over a hot spot when magma rose through the crust. Hawaii is on the Pacific plate. The plate is always moving. Most scientists believe Hawaii formed into a chain of islands as the Pacific plate moved over a magma hot spot. Magma that reaches Earth's surface is called lava. As lava explodes or flows from Earth's crust, it often forms peaks, called volcanoes. The world's biggest volcano, Mauna Loa, is in the Hawaiian Islands.

Yellowstone National Park, Wyoming, in the Rocky Mountains has more geysers than anywhere else in the world. Old Faithful Geyser shoots boiling water up to 180 feet (55 meters) into the air about every ninety minutes.

## Heating the water

Mostly, magma stays underground. It heats the rocks that form the crust. It also heats any water, called groundwater, that flows through these rocks. Most of this groundwater comes from rain or melted snow that seeps into the ground. The water makes its way deep into the crust through cracks and channels.

Groundwater heated by hot spots is known as **geothermal water**. It can reach temperatures above 212 °F (100 °C). This is the normal boiling point of water. High pressure underground prevents the water from boiling. Sometimes, the hot water bubbles out of the ground as a hot spring. In other places, it bursts out of the ground and instantly changes into steam. The hot water and steam form a fountain called a **geyser**. More often, geothermal water stays in the ground, trapped in rocks.

How can we use the heat energy stored underground? People have found several ways. At hot spots, hot water can be pumped out of the ground. But heat energy can also be pumped out even where there is no geothermal water. Earth's stored heat can be drawn from the ground itself.

## KEY WORDS

**core:** the innermost layer of Earth
**crust:** the rocky outer layer of Earth
**hot spot:** a place where magma sometimes breaks through Earth's crust
**mantle:** the semi-solid layer between Earth's crust and core

# CHAPTER THREE

# HEAT FROM THE GROUND

Hot springs and pools form if geothermal water reaches the surface. In several areas of the world, people use this water for cooking and heating. This is called **direct use** of geothermal energy. Water temperatures must be between 50 °F (10 °C) and 300 °F (150 °C) for such use.

## Drilling deep

Engineers drill a **borehole** to reach geothermal water in underground rock. Sometimes, the water is several thousand feet (meters) deep. When geothermal water is reached, a steel pipe (called the casing) is lowered into the borehole. Holes in the casing let the geothermal water into the pipe.

Geothermal water is often under enough pressure to flow up the pipe to the surface on its own. But sometimes the water must be pumped out.

## Heat exchange

Often, geothermal water cannot be used directly from the ground. It may contain dissolved substances that are poisonous or can damage pipes. A device called a **heat exchanger** is used to transfer heat from geothermal water to clean water. Clean water is pumped through a separate set of pipes next to the pipes that hold the geothermal water. The clean water absorbs the heat. This is pumped to the area that

## HOT SPRINGS

Hot springs and pools form where geothermal water bubbles up onto the surface. For thousands of years, people have used these thermal features for cooking, bathing, and heating. The ancient Romans liked to have hot baths. They built large bath houses where people could bathe and relax. In what is now Bath, England, people still like to bathe in hot spring water. (Bath was the ancient Roman town called Aquae Sulis.) Many believe such bathing cures certain health problems.

Valley View Hot Springs, Colorado, is one of several natural geothermal pools in the United States.

needs heating. Geothermal water is returned to the ground for eventual reuse.

### Farm and industrial use

Geothermal heat can be used to keep greenhouses warm. Plants grow more quickly when they are warm. Geothermal water is also often used for fish farms. Many fish grow faster in warm water than in cold water. Less time is needed

Reykjavik, Iceland, began using geothermal district heating in 1930. Today, about 90 percent of Icelanders use geothermal heating or electricity.

for the fish to grow large enough to sell.

The food processing industry uses geothermal energy to process and cook food. Concrete and timber businesses use geothermal heat to dry their products. The heat is also used for making paper and dyeing fabrics.

## Heating buildings

Hot water piped into buildings can provide heat. Geothermal heat can warm a single building or can even warm many city blocks.

Iceland's capital city, Reykjavik, uses geothermal heat. (The name "Reykjavik" means "smoky bay" because of its steaming landscape.) Reykjavik and surrounding areas have the world's largest geothermal **district heating** system. Reykjavik was once heavily polluted. Thanks to geothermal energy, Reykjavik is now one of the world's cleanest cities.

## Geothermal heat pumps

Everywhere on Earth, not too far below the surface, the ground stays at about 50 °F (10 °C) all year. This steady temperature can be used to heat buildings in winter. It can also cool buildings in summer. A device called a **heat pump** lets us use this geothermal energy.

In a heat pump, a long tube is buried underground. Liquid is pumped through it. The liquid draws heat from the ground and transfers it to the building above. In summer, the heat pump transfers excess heat to the ground and keeps the building cool.

Heat pumps work anywhere. You do not need to be near a source of geothermal water or steam. More than 350,000 buildings in the United States use geothermal heat pumps.

### USES FOR GEOTHERMAL HEAT

Percentage of total use

| | |
|---|---|
| heat pumps | 71.12 |
| fish farming | 9.64 |
| bathing and swimming | 8.14 |
| heating single buildings | 4.27 |
| district heating | 2.52 |
| heating greenhouses | 2.45 |
| agricultural drying | 1.60 |
| industrial processes | 0.15 |
| melting snow | 0.06 |
| cooling structures | 0.05 |

Most of the world's geothermal energy use helps power geothermal heat pumps.

### KEY WORDS

**direct use:** using geothermal energy without converting it into electricity
**district heating:** a single-source heating system that heats a full block or an even larger area of a city
**heat pump:** a machine that moves heat energy from one place to another

# CHAPTER FOUR

# ELECTRICITY FROM STEAM

**P**ower plants all work the same basic way. They use steam to produce electricity. Steam, which is a clear, colorless gas, pushes against the blades of a **turbine**. A turbine has blades that spin around. The spinning turbine blades turn a shaft called a rotor. The spinning rotor is part of a machine called a **generator,** which generates electricity.

Most power plants create steam by burning fossil fuels. More than twenty countries have geothermal power plants, however.

The United States, the Philippines, Italy, and Mexico produce the most geothermal electricity. The United States makes nearly one-third of the world's geothermal electricity. California produces about 88 percent of the geothermal electricity in the United States. Nevada produces about 10 percent of this share. Hawaii and Utah each produce about 1 percent.

About half of the geothermal energy used around the world is used for producing electricity. Geothermal power plants must be located over a source of very hot water or steam. Boreholes drilled into the ground reach the geothermal source. The steam or water travels to the surface for use in the power plant. There are several different kinds of geothermal power plants. They include dry steam,

# THE BLUE LAGOON

Iceland has several geothermal power plants. One of these is Svartsengi, a combined heat and power plant. This kind of plant makes electrical power and supplies heat to buildings. The plant at Svartsengi has also become a popular resort! A created lake, called the Blue Lagoon, holds geothermal water from the power plant. Svartsengi's geothermal water is very clean. It is rich with minerals that people believe are good for their health. Many people come to the Blue Lagoon to soak and swim in the warm, soothing waters.

The Blue Lagoon is a popular spa in Svartsengi, Iceland. It is a clever use of wastewater from the geothermal power plant.

## DRILLING A BOREHOLE

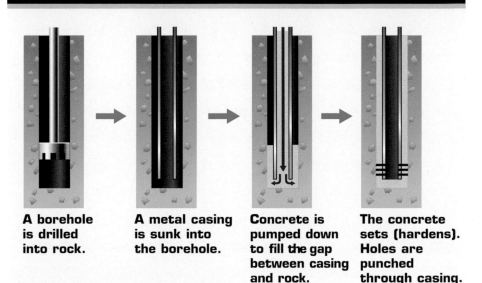

**A borehole is drilled into rock.**

**A metal casing is sunk into the borehole.**

**Concrete is pumped down to fill the gap between casing and rock.**

**The concrete sets (hardens). Holes are punched through casing.**

A geothermal borehole is created in several steps. A special "gun" punches holes through the metal casing and concrete. This allows the steam or hot water to pass through.

flashed steam, **binary,** and **hybrid power plants.**

### Dry steam plants

Some geothermal sources do not produce lots of hot water. They produce dry steam instead. This is steam mixed with only a very little water. Dry steam plants use these sources for power.

The world's first dry steam power plant opened at Larderello, Italy, in 1904. At first, it produced enough electricity for just five electric lightbulbs. Today, Larderello makes about 10 percent of the world's geothermal electricity — enough for one million homes.

## THE GEYSERS

The Geysers dry steam field in Sonoma County, California, is the largest producer of geothermal electricity in the world. The first geothermal power plant in the United States opened there in 1960. Twenty-one plants are working at The Geysers now. They make enough electricity for 750,000 homes.

In the 1990s, the output of steam at The Geysers fell. Steam was being used faster than it was being replaced. Rainwater trickling into the ground was not keeping up with steam being removed. Since 2003, wastewater from nearby towns has been pumped into the ground. This makes more steam for the power plants. Some people are worried that injecting water will cause small earthquakes. The water might open up cracks in the rocks when it boils. Scientists monitor (check) the area for signs of earthquakes.

The Geysers power plant, with a 750-megawatt output, is the largest producer of geothermal power in the world.

## Flashed steam plants

Dry steam **power plants** do not work if the geothermal source produces hot water instead of steam. Flashed steam plants are the most common type of geothermal power plant. The water deep below the surface is under pressure. It stays liquid, even though it is much hotter than water's boiling point. When it reaches the surface, some of the hot water "flashes." This means it instantly boils (turns to gas, or steam). The steam spins a turbine, which turns a generator.

No steam escapes from the generator. Instead, it is cooled so that it **condenses** (turns back into liquid water). The water is pumped back into the hot rocks to be heated again. Recycling the water in this way keeps the pressure underground high. It also ensures that the power plant does not run out of water.

## Binary power plants

Many sources of geothermal water are not hot enough for a flashed steam plant to work. A binary power plant is used instead. Binary means having two parts. A binary plant uses two liquids, not just the geothermal water.

The geothermal water is brought to the surface. Its heat warms a second liquid in separate pipes. This second, "binary liquid" is usually a chemical with a lower boiling point than water. Water boils at 212 °F (100 °C). But a liquid called methylbutane boils at just 82 °F (28 °C). It easily turns into a gas when it is warmed by geothermal water and powers a turbine, which turns a generator. The gas is

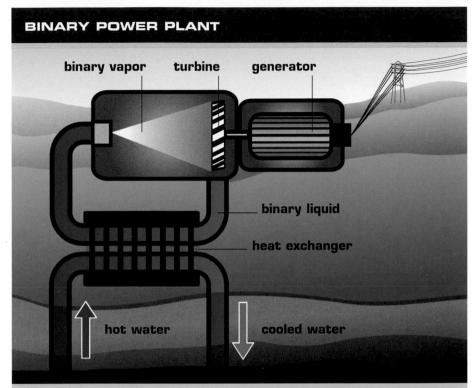

## BINARY POWER PLANT

binary vapor    turbine    generator

binary liquid

heat exchanger

hot water    cooled water

Binary power plants use lower-temperature water to make electricity. This design allows for wider use of geothermal energy for power production.

then cooled down so it condenses back to a liquid. The geothermal water and methylbutane are recycled.

A hybrid power plant combines the flash and binary processes. The "big" island of Hawaii gets one-fourth of its electricity from a hybrid power plant.

## KEY WORDS

**binary power plant:** a plant that produces electricity using two liquids
**hybrid power plant:** a plant that produces electricity by combining two processes
**power plant:** a factory that produces electricity, usually for a wide area

# CHAPTER FIVE

# THE GEOTHERMAL FUTURE

The world faces many problems with its energy supply. We know fossil fuels will run out one day. These fuels also cause pollution and global warming.

Geothermal sources do release some carbon dioxide. But they release about a thousand times less carbon dioxide than fossil fuels to make the same amount of heat. Can geothermal energy help us in the future?

## In the United States

In the western United States, there are thousands of potential geothermal sources. Nearly one thousand places have geothermal water that is warm enough to be useful. In the West, more than seven million people in 271 communities are close to useful geothermal sources. For those people, it could be five times cheaper to heat a building with geothermal energy than with fossil fuels.

Even if we use all these hot springs, there will still be a huge amount of geothermal energy left in the ground. Will it be possible to use more of this energy? Geothermal heat pumps can draw heat from the ground anywhere. These pumps can even be installed in a small backyard. In the future, almost everyone could heat and cool their homes with geothermal heat pumps.

> "We know very well that we're . . . sitting on a virtually inexhaustible supply of geothermal energy and choosing instead to transport oil, gas, and coal over thousands of kilometers rather than digging a few kilometers into the Earth."

Willy Gehrer, president of the energy company ETG Electrosuisse in Switzerland, speaking in 2004

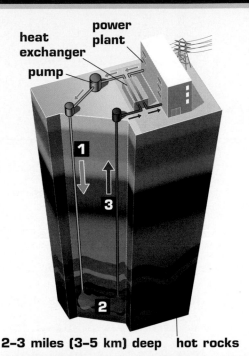

heat exchanger
power plant
pump

**1**
**3**
**2**

**2–3 miles (3–5 km) deep    hot rocks**

Cold water is pumped down [1]. The cold water is warmed by the hot rocks [2]. Hot, geothermal water returns to the surface [3].

## Hot dry rocks

Very hot water or steam is needed for generating electricity. Today's geothermal power plants can only be built over a source of very hot water or steam. Most parts of the world cannot use geothermal power plants. In the future, however, geothermal plants could be everywhere. These plants of the future would use **hot dry-rock energy**. This is the natural heat energy found deep in the rock layers everywhere on Earth. It does not depend on a geothermal hot spot.

## THE DEEPEST HOLE

The deepest hole ever drilled is the Kola Superdeep Borehole. It is in Russia, near the border with Norway. Drilling started in 1970. Scientists wanted to find out more about Earth's crust. After twenty-four years of drilling, the borehole reached more than 7.5 miles (12 km) into Earth's crust. It became too hot at the bottom of the hole for drilling to continue. The work stopped in 1994.

Rocks get hotter the deeper underground you go. A few miles (km) down, they may be as hot as 400 °F (200 °C). If we drill down to these rocks, we can get large amounts of geothermal heat.

How do engineers bring the heat energy out of the rocks? They make their own geothermal water. First, cold water is pumped down a borehole into the hot rock. It flows through cracks in the rock and is heated up. Hot water returns to the surface through another borehole. It can be used just like geothermal water that was made naturally. The water is recycled back to the hot rocks, and no pollution is caused.

It is expensive to drill the deep boreholes needed for hot dry-rock energy. Oil and gas industries already drill deep holes like these. So, we already have the drilling technology to create such deep boreholes. In Texas alone, there are more than

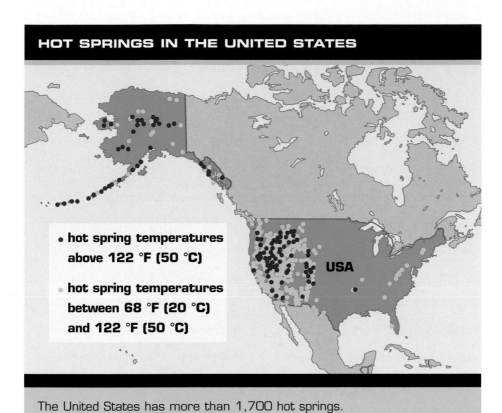

## HOT SPRINGS IN THE UNITED STATES

• hot spring temperatures above 122 °F (50 °C)

• hot spring temperatures between 68 °F (20 °C) and 122 °F (50 °C)

USA

The United States has more than 1,700 hot springs.

half a million oil wells. Many of these reach deeper than the boreholes needed for geothermal energy.

Geothermal energy has a bright future. Some scientists believe that geothermal energy might provide as much as 10 percent of the United States' energy supply of the future. Depending on where you live, it may be part of your life already.

Sooner or later, everybody will benefit from the energy under our feet.

## KEY WORDS

**hot dry-rock energy:** heat energy taken from hot rocks deep underground

# GLOSSARY

**borehole:** a hole drilled into Earth's crust

**condense:** to change from a gas into a liquid

**elastic energy:** potential energy — energy stored in an object because of its position

**emissions:** waste substances, such as carbon dioxide, given off by fossil fuel burning and other processes

**generator:** a machine that changes mechanical energy into electrical energy

**geothermal energy:** heat energy from inside Earth

**geothermal water:** groundwater heated by Earth's natural heat

**geyser:** a natural, hot, underground spring that sprays hot water and steam into the air

**heat exchanger:** a system in which heat passes from one substance to another without them mixing

**hot dry-rock energy:** heat energy taken from hot rock layers deep underground

**hot spot:** a place where magma sometimes breaks through Earth's crust

**nuclear reaction:** a change that breaks apart an atom's nucleus to create energy

**power plant:** a factory that produces electricity

**tectonic plates:** large pieces of crust and upper mantle

**turbine:** a type of engine powered by a flow of fluid. A turbine has large blades that spin and power a shaft, or rotor, on a generator, which creates electricity.

# TOP EIGHT ENERGY SOURCES

### in alphabetical order

The following list highlights the major fuel sources of the twenty-first century.
It also lists some advantages and disadvantages of each:

| | Advantages | Disadvantages |
|---|---|---|
| **Biofuels** | renewable energy source; widely available from a number of sources, including farms, restaurants, and everday garbage | fossil fuels often used to grow farm crops; requires special processing facilities that run on fossil fuels in order to produce usable biofuel |
| **Fossil fuels: coal, oil, petroleum** | used by functioning power plants worldwide; supports economies | limited supplies; emit greenhouse gases; produce toxic wastes; must often be transported long distances |
| **Geothermal energy** | nonpolluting; renewable; free source | only available in localized areas; would require redesign of heating systems |
| **Hydrogen (fuel cells)** | most abundant element in the universe; nonpolluting | fuel cell production uses up fossil fuels; hydrogen gas storage presents safety issues |
| **Nuclear energy** | produces no greenhouse gases; produces a lot of energy from small amounts of fuel | solid wastes remain dangerous for centuries; limited life span of power plants |
| **Solar power** | renewable; produces no pollutants; free source | weather and climate dependent; solar cells expensive to manufacture |
| **Water power** | renewable resource; generally requires no additional fuel | requires flowing water, waves, or tides; can interfere with view; dams may destroy large natural areas and disrupt human settlements |
| **Wind power** | renewable; nonpolluting; free source | depends on weather patterns; depends on location; endangers bird populations |

# RESOURCES

## Books

Morris, Neil.
*Geothermal Power.*
Energy Sources (series).
Smart Apple Media (2006)

Saunders, Nigel and Steve Chapman.
*Renewable Energy.*
Energy Essentials (series).
Raintree (2005)

## Web Sites

*www.eia.doe.gov/kids/energyfacts/
sources/renewable/geothermal.html*
Explore the world's "ring of fire" on
the Department of Energy Web site.

*www.energyquest.ca.gov/story/
chapter11.html*
Visit the California Energy
Commission's educational Web site
for geothermal energy.

**Publisher's note to educators and parents:** Our editors have carefully reviewed these
Web sites to ensure that they are suitable for children. Many Web sites change
frequently, however, and we cannot guarantee that a site's future contents will
continue to meet our high standards of quality and educational value. Be advised
that children should be closely supervised whenever they access the Internet.

# INDEX